SHORT · SCENIC · WALKS

SEDBERGH & Dentdale

PAUL HANNON

HILLSIDE PUBLICATIONS
20 Wheathead Crescent
Keighley
West Yorkshire
BD22 6LX

First Published 2010

ISBN 978 1 907626 05 0

While the author has walked and researched all these routes for the purposes of this guide, no responsibility can be accepted for any unforeseen circumstances encountered whilst following them

The sketch maps are based on 1947 OS one-inch maps and earlier OS six-inch maps

Cover illustration: The Howgill Fells from above Dowbiggin
Back cover: Dentdale
Page 1: The cobbled streets of Dent
(Paul Hannon/Hillslides Picture Library)

Printed by Steffprint
Unit 5, Keighley Industrial Park
Royd Ings Avenue
Keighley
West Yorkshire
BD21 4DZ

CONTENTS

INTRODUCTION

The north-western corner of the Yorkshire Dales is undoubtedly the least visited, yet it offers outstanding walking amid the most exquisite scenery, a stunning mix of fells, foothills, rolling pastures and lush riverbanks. At the very heart of this sparsely populated district is Sedbergh, a smashing little town which is the largest community in the National Park. It occupies an idyllic position at the base of the Howgill Fells, and presides over the convergence of the area's many rivers. Home to a famous public school, it is also making ambitious strides as England's 'Book Town', an admirable asset that dovetails with the peaceful ambience of the locality.

The only other community of any size is Dent, an enchanting little place midway along beautiful Dentdale. Its river the Dee flows through neat sheep pastures towards Sedbergh, as does the little known River Clough that runs a parallel journey through neighbouring Garsdale. The River Rawthey, meanwhile, absorbs both on its delectable course from near the lonely summit of Baugh Fell to Sedbergh. It demarcates the eastern boundary of the Howgill Fells in similar fashion to the Lune on their western side, and it is the Lune which it joins beyond Sedbergh.

The inimitable Howgills are invariably in evidence on most forays hereabouts. These fine grassy hills form a compact group that offers endless scope for bracing walks. Rarely in evidence is the underlying slate, though when revealed it is in some style, at the remarkable ravines of Cautley and Carlingill. The entire area falls within Cumbria, though until 1974 it was part of Yorkshire's West Riding. A little further afield are the market towns of Kirkby Stephen and Hawes, while the nearest large town is Kendal.

Most of the walks are on rights of way with no access restrictions. Some also make use of 'Right to Roam' to cross Open Country: these areas can be closed for up to 28 days each year subject to advance notice, though they are almost entirely within the Howgill Fells which have enjoyed open access since time immemorial. Whilst the route description should be sufficient to guide you around each walk, a map is recommended for greater information: Ordnance Survey 1:25,000 scale maps give the finest detail, and Explorers OL2 and OL19 cover all of the walks.

Carlingill

USEFUL INFORMATION

·Yorkshire Dales National Park (01756-751600)
·Sedbergh Tourist Information (015396-20125)
·Hawes National Park Centre (01969-666210)
·Kirkby Stephen Tourist Information (017683-71199)
·Open Access (0845-100 3298) www.countrysideaccess.gov.uk
·Traveline - public transport information (0870-6082608)

SEDBERGH & Dentdale

20 Short Scenic Walks

Church Bridge, Dent

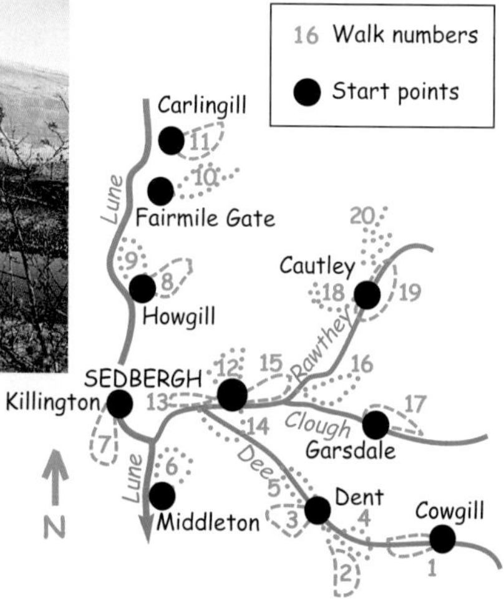

Fell pony on the Howgills

A RECORD OF YOUR WALKS

WALK	DATE	NOTES
1		
2		
3		
4		
5		
6		
7		
8		
9		
10		
11		
12		
13		
14		
15		
16		
17		
18		
19		
20		

1 Upper Dentdale

4½ miles from Cowgill

Lovely rambling through endless sheep pastures above the Dee

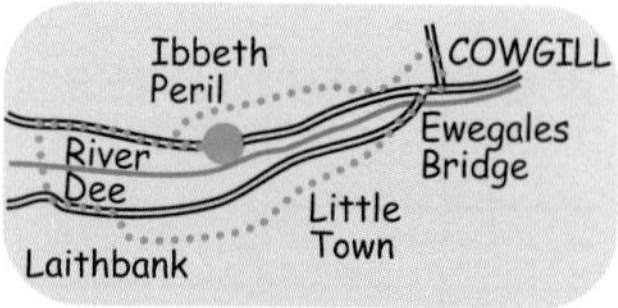

Start *Ibbeth Peril (GR: 741864), car park mile west of church*
Map *OS Explorer OL2, Yorkshire Dales South/West*

A path runs downstream through trees to look down on Ibbeth Peril waterfall, assuming the Dee is not in one of its dry spells! A little further is an option to appraise the scene from the riverbed, beneath limestone walls. Returning to the road near a milestone head down-dale, rising above the river as far as a drive on the right. Turn up this as it doubles back up to Broadfield House. Pass along the front and over a bridge to the next one, where a gate sends you round the back. A stile crosses another stream to derelict Blands. Just before it a gate sends you down a green way to a barn: from a gate to its left enter a field. Cross to a gateway and on a field top to a barn and a drive. Cross onto a lesser track bridging a wooded gill, and rising into a field cross to a stile ahead, revealing Hollins in front. Widdale Fell fills the dalehead skyline. Advance to the buildings, through a stile above and on to the end to drop into the yard, home to Dent Brewery.

From a gate in front a track rises to a cottage, continue to a corner gate. Advance to the drive to Broadmire above. Turn briefly right down this, but as it turns down to the road take a stile ahead, over a stream onto another drive beneath a house. Cross straight over to a stile onto another slab bridge on a tree-lined stream, and pass between barns to Spice Gill farmhouse. Go left along the front and on past a couple of barns to a gate/stile into a field. Go straight across to another slab bridge onto a farm track, across which trace a wall-side to a corner stile. Now bear right to a corner stile at the rear of roadside buildings. Resume by bearing left to a nice corner with slab bridge and stile, then on through a gateway left of a barn to a small gate onto a drive. Cross and follow the wall away to a corner stile. Bear left to a stile onto a green lane: go right over Dockra Bridge on Cowgill Beck. Becoming surfaced it drops down to St John's church, Cowgill.

Turn right then left over Ewegales Bridge on a back road: shortly after Ewegales Farm take a gate on the left and along a drive to Rivling. Pass beneath the buildings to a stile into a plantation, scene of large-scale felling in 2010. A path runs on to approach Little Town, then drops right to a small gate onto a drive. Cross a drive beyond it and pass right of buildings to a stile into the second half of the trees. A level path runs to adjacent stiles to escape, continuing by a wall to a corner stile onto Birchen Tree's drive. Rise briefly up it then cross to a stile opposite. A thin path contours left to a gate/stile onto another drive: turn left. With Hackergill above, fork right over a bridge to a stile on the right at Coat Faw. From it cross to one to the left, then right with the wall beneath a limestone scar. Approaching Clint you are deflected above it and on to a stile and plank bridge to approach West Clint. Rise Hill's slopes overtop the fields across the valley. Go left into the farmyard and pass the house front, continuing out on the rough drive. When it turns downhill take a stile in front, on to meet yet another drive by a barn beneath white-walled Swarthwaite.

Cross straight over and across the field to a plank bridge on a tree-lined gill. Just beyond it pass right of a large barn, and from a stile behind it join Laithbank's drive. Turn down it to the road and go left until just past the first house, then take a gate on the right. Drop to Tub Hole, a wooded ravine: usually dry, the resurgence can be substantial just prior to meeting the Dee. Pass to the right to meet the often-dry Dee at Nelly Bridge. Across, bear left up to a gate onto the road at Basil Busk. Turn right to finish, passing Gibbs Hall en route: the ruin of the old hall stands alongside.

Ibbeth Peril

2 DEEPDALE

3¼ miles from Dent

Exploring a beautiful and remote offshoot of Dentdale

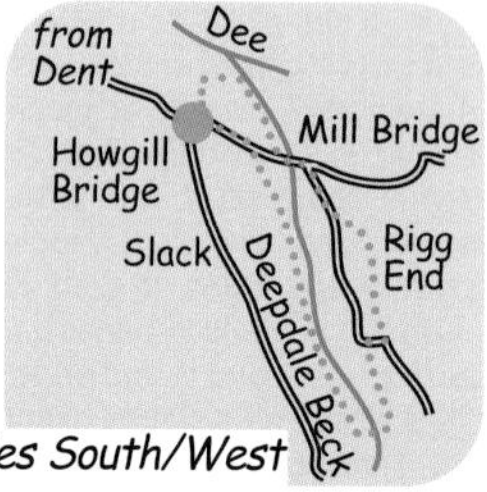

Start Howgill Bridge (GR: 714862) limited parking a mile east of Dent, by phone box and on Dent approach
Map OS Explorer OL2, Yorkshire Dales South/West

Head east on the road (away from Dent) the short way to a junction: a seat enjoys massive Dentdale views, from Widdale Fell down to the Howgill Fells. Go left here down an enclosed cart track to idyllically sited Double Croft. While the bridleway goes straight on, take a stile on the right just before the house. Cross the fieldside to a path by often-dry Deepdale Beck, and turn right to shadow it upstream to Mill Bridge. Emerging via trees onto the road, go left over the bridge and rise outside a plantation to a fork: branch right here at a tiny Methodist chapel, the entrance to Deepdale. The road climbs to reveal Deepdale outspread. This is the only real break in Dentdale's steep valley sides: Deepdale Beck flows for no more than three miles in its entirety, but creates a deep-cut side valley which is very much a chip off the old block. Its farms are dotted about the lush pastures in a virtual time capsule.

Levelling out as an enclosed track (Craven Way) turns off left, within a minute leave by a gate on the left. Bear right across unkempt pasture, slanting above a stone hut and on through a line of gnarled trees. Continue slanting to a stile in a short length of wall near the top. Advance across a field-top to approach Rigg End: Great Coum appears massive above Deepdale's fields. Looking back down-dale are the Howgills, with nearer Combe Scar to the left and Rise Hill right. Pass along the front outside the farm, over the drive to a gate in the wall ahead. Head directly away, dropping slightly to a wall-stile ahead. On view is a Deepdale horseshoe including Whernside and Great Coum. Drop down through a gateway to rejoin the road, now a concrete track: on your left is an old limekiln.

Turn right down the road just as far as a sharp bend right. From a gate on the left cross a field-top to a stile in a tiny section of wall above a wooded bank of Deepdale Beck. From a stile at the end of the trees drop down across a large sloping pasture, crossing a small stream midway and continuing to a stile in a tiny section of wall beneath a barn. Cross a slab bridge behind and from a kissing-gate advance to a stile and a tiny, tree-lined stream. This time slant down the field to a farm bridge on the beck flowing over limestone slabs. Across, ascend a rough track by the fence to a corner gate just above. Through this begin a long march downstream along the valley floor. Head away, on through two further gates from where a wall guides the old way along to a barn. While a path branches up left, take the briefly enclosed green way curving down to the beck. In this lovely spot amid trees the beck tumbles over rocky slabs.

Ignoring a footbridge remain on this bank and head off downstream, commencing a lengthy section close by the lively beck. Through a wall-stile immediately beneath the farm of Scow, quickly bear left of a small plantation to leave the beck. Bear slightly left to a path junction at a stile with an old limekiln behind. Advance on by a scrubby bank and rise slightly to an old stile ahead, then cross a longer pasture to a kissing-gate in a wall. Through this advance on to a corner gate to join a back road. Go left past cottages and Cage Farm, rising sharply back to the junction near the start.

Deepdale Beck

3 FLINTER GILL

4 miles from Dent

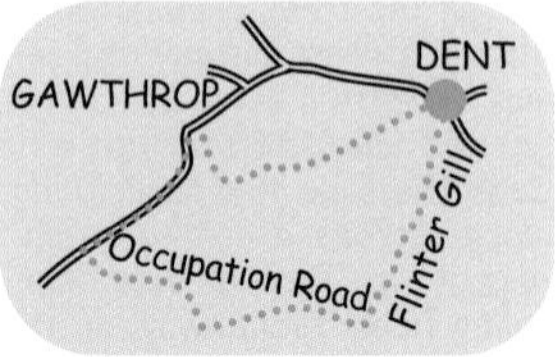

A steep, leafy gill leads to a bracing stride with big views

Start Village centre (GR: 704870), car park
Map OS Explorer OL2, Yorkshire Dales South/West

From the car park cross the road to one rising past the school and green. A nice group of cottages and a Zion Chapel (1835) precede the start of Flinter Gill. At the last cottage a stony track takes over to begin its climb above the beck. In its enchanting setting the stream tumbles over a series of rock ledges in a deep, wooded ravine, though after a dry spell it may be conspicuous by its absence. Various features punctuate this steep, stony climb. Immediately on the left are the Dancing Slabs, flat rocks used by weavers for dampening and trampling on their cloth to improve it! Then follows the intriguingly knotted trunk of the Wishing Tree. Higher, a gate on the right gives access to High Ground Farmstead just behind, which proves to be a restored barn containing a small museum of farming implements. Back on route you pass a restored limekiln, with a small old quarry behind it by the shelved beck.

Near the top of the gill the way emerges from wooded confines and the gradients finally ease. A stile on the right just before a gate gives access to a toposcope detailing the magnificent view: on parade is a great sweep of Dentdale leading down to the Howgill Fells across the foot of the valley. Largely enclosed by walls but easier underfoot, the way rises to join an enclosed track, the Occupation Road. A beautifully composed scene awaits as lower Dentdale leads the eye to the Howgills. This old packhorse way and service road for the enclosures runs across the northern flank of Great Coum, and provides marvellous sweeping views over the dale. Turn right along its wide course for a long, elevated stride. Soon reaching your high point at around 1180ft/360m, the way gradually curves around and down to eventually meet the Dent-Barbon road.

Accompany the road right, gently to its summit on Stone Rigg. Looking back, Great Coum forms a long, flat skyline. The road soon drops sharply, and opens out beneath a narrow bend: take a gate on the right where an access track heads off. This runs to cross a wooded gill and back out to run on to High House Farm. Pass left of all buildings and around the back, where you see the house 'front' with a 17th century datestone above an arch-headed window. From a stile on the left slant down a wooded bank, then briefly upstream to a slab footbridge. A path doubles back up to a stile out, then cross to one at the far left corner of the field. From a ladder-stile behind it drop to one in the far corner. Over a trickle cross to another and bear left to a stile with an old gap-stile just below.

Dent has by now returned to the scene beneath up-dale views to Widdale Fell and Whernside. Drop down the hedgeside to a gate/stile in the corner, then down onto a track just short of the farm at Mill Beck. Pass through and remain on the main track the full length of the buildings and out into a field at the end. Drop down to the left to the right-hand of two corner gates, and cross a field bottom to a stile in front of a very large modern barn. Pass to its left alongside a caravan field at High Laning Farm. Head right towards the yard, and then out along its drive to emerge onto the road through Dent adjacent to a Methodist Chapel of 1834.

Dent and Rise Hill from Flinter Gill

4 THE DEE ABOVE DENT

3½ miles from Dent

Very easy rambling on and around the banks of the Dee upstream of Dent

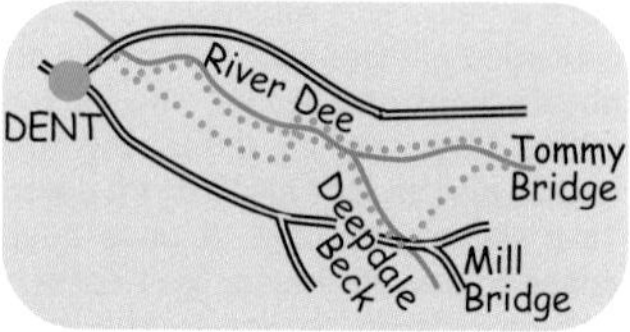

Start Village centre (GR: 704870), car park
Map OS Explorer OL2, Yorkshire Dales South/West

For a note on Dent see page 16. From the car park head along the cobbled street in the village centre, keeping left to drop down to Church Bridge. Across the valley is Rise Hill, up the dale rises Whernside, while back over the village is Great Coum. Don't cross the bridge but take a path on the right and head away upstream, immediately deflected from the Dee by the smaller Keld Beck. Follow this just as far as a farm bridge on it, across which cross to a wall just ahead and then bear right with this as it guides a path curving back to the river. Now simply head upstream on a well-used, largely enclosed path faithfully shadowing the enchanting Dee. Keep straight on the riverbank at a junction with a bridleway at a concrete ford and stepping-stones: you will return to this point later, so it's worth a glance to see that the stepping-stones will be passable. Ahead, mighty Whernside encloses Deepdale.

Just two minutes beyond the ford you reach a major confluence with Deepdale Beck. This is a lovely spot which deserves a pause, even though the side beck can often be entirely dry here. Deepdale Beck - or at least its deep course - is now your companion all the way to Mill Bridge, where you emerge via trees onto a road. Go left over the bridge and take a ladder-stile alongside the house at Bridge End. Rise left up the field to a wall corner, then over the domed brow: ahead, Widdale Fell and Dent Station are seen further up-dale. At a lone Scots pine is another wall corner, and a path drops down to a gap-stile below to rejoin the river. Turn upstream the short way to the footbridge of Tommy Bridge. Across, double back downstream and the path now clings to the riverbank for rather less than a mile enjoying some very good river scenery. The confluence with Deepdale Beck is passed, possibly unnoticed, just before reaching the ford and sturdy stepping-stones from earlier. If impassable, turn right to a bridle-gate where a short-lived enclosed way joins the road at Scotchergill Bridge, going left to follow this back to Dent.

Assuming you've crossed, simplest option is to trace the outward riverbank route back to Church Bridge. For more variety however, advance straight on the sunken bridleway heading away from the river to the idyllically sited house at Double Croft. While the bridleway advances straight on, your way takes a stile on the right immediately after the house. Cross the field to another stile beyond the house, and advance along a briefly enclosed green way. Through a gate at the end continue on with a hedge on your left, and keep on to find a stile at the very end. From here a clear path shadows a tiny beck through scrub, leaving by a stile just before the end. In front a gate/stile point to a ford/stepping-stones on the larger Keld Beck just above, but your way takes the adjacent stile and crosses to one in the corner just beyond. Here a splendid enclosed path shadows Keld Beck back to the farm bridge near the start. Cross it and retrace the opening steps back to Church Bridge, just ahead.

The River Dee above Dent

5 The Dee below Dent

4¾ miles from Dent

An utterly delightful, low-level riverbank stroll

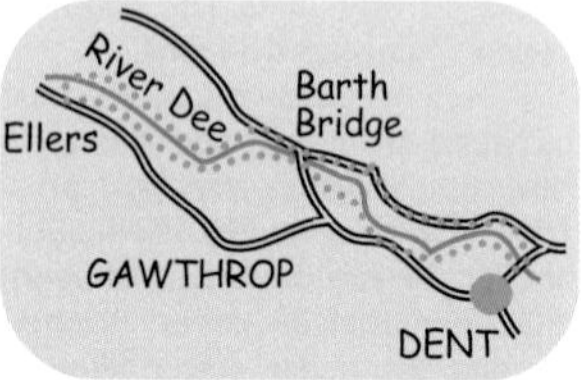

Start *Village centre (GR: 704870), car park*
Map *OS Explorer OL2, Yorkshire Dales South/West*

Dent is only a village in size, but is still known as Dent Town in recognition of once greater importance. Today it is an unhurried backwater midway along its own valley: the only roads in and out are minor ones, a factor which has helped preserve Dent's character. Retained are some cobbled streets lined with neat cottages, a Post office/shop, cafés and a pair of pubs. St Andrew's church dates in part from the 15th century: the tower dates from the late 18th century. Between the Sun Inn and the George & Dragon is a block of Shap granite serving as a drinking fountain, and carved with the name Adam Sedgwick. Born here in 1785, he spent over 50 years as Professor of Geology at Cambridge. One of the earliest and best in his field, he did much research into the fascinating geology of his own back yard. At least one of the pubs serves ale brewed just up the road in this very dale: support a local industry and savour an excellent product at the same time! Also here are a Methodist church built as a Wesleyan Chapel in 1834, a Zion Chapel of 1835 that now serves as a meditation centre, and a Reading Room of 1880. A heritage centre gives an excellent picture of the area in times past, while the National School of 1845 still serves the dale's youngsters.

From the car park head along the cobbled street in the village centre, keeping left to drop down to Church Bridge. Don't use it but take a stile on the left to descend to the river. Virtually at once there is a fine prospect of Dent under the slopes of Great Coum. The Dee is hugged all the way to the walk's turning point, the footbridge at Ellers. The only breaks are early on, when the river nudges you onto a hundred yards of road, and approaching Barth Bridge, where gates take a more direct course onto the road. The riverbank path resumes across the road. The crystal-clear Dee is in sedate mood, this outward bank being especially beautiful backed by the colourful hollow of Combe Scar towering over the walk.

In a final tapering field, with the cottage at Ellers ahead, the path is sent left across the field to a stile onto a back road. Go right on it the short way to the footbridge and ford by the cottage. Cross the bridge and set off back along the other bank, this lengthy section being entirely on the crest of a flood embankment. Rise Hill fills the valley side to the left, with Whernside ahead. At the end a wooded bank forces you up onto the road at a monument. The Elam Monument is a tablet honouring Lucy Elam, who in 1876 footed the bill for a re-routing of this section of road. Turn right to arrive back at Barth Bridge. To savour more of the riverbank cross and retrace the opening mile. For the circular route remain on this bank on Hall Lane. This gem of a traffic-free way is wrapped within some colourful hedgerows, initially by the river. Later, not long after passing the attractive, white-walled Low Hall, a stile returns you to the riverbank for the final field back to steps and a stile up onto Church Bridge.

The Dee near Ellers

6 HOLME KNOTT

3¾ miles from Middleton

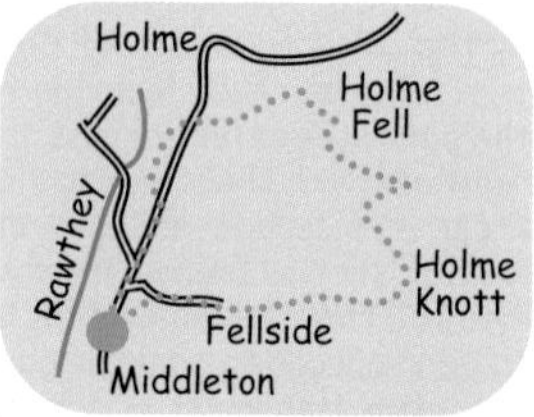

A truly delightful walk over a classic little fell with stunning views of the Sedbergh scene

Start The Head pub (GR: 629886), lay-by to north
Map OS Explorer OL2, Yorkshire Dales South/West
OS Explorer OL19, Howgill Fells & Upper Eden Valley
Access Open Access, see page 5

Between the lay-by and the pub a track rises into a sliver of woodland. Climbing away, it eases out to run a broad enclosed course left between scattered trees. Above is the knobbly skyline of Holme Knott, with the Howgill Fells ahead. At the end an access road is joined and leads right through open country up to a house at Fellside. Pass through a gate ahead and a grass track heads off along the length of a pasture. Through the left-hand of two gates at the end Open Country is entered. The inviting track heads away, rising gently through part bracken slopes. Up ahead to the right are slopes rising to Calf Top. Fording a colourful stream the way forks.

Take the left branch climbing by the slabby stream then veering away. At the top it reaches a level platform on a minor bank, then bears right to run level to a lesser stream. Instead of crossing take a more inviting branch doubling back left. This rises then runs on to ford a small stream. It rises away as a super green track to meet the main stream from earlier, now tamely emerging from the moss on your right. A couple of minutes further is a cross-tracks just short of a brow. Turn right to ascend Holme Knott, rising beneath minor outcrops to a saddle revealing an awesome prospect of the Howgill Fells. When the track drops away turn right on a thin trod up to the Ordnance Survey column at 1148ft/350m on a minor ridge, revealing a tarn at your feet. Sedbergh is now suitably placed beneath the Howgills: elsewehere the Lune Valley leads south towards Bowland, Wild Boar, Swarth and Baugh Fells rise across the Rawthey, while a clear day reveals a Lakeland skyline. Holme Knott itself also has further interest with three knolls across the saddle.

Resume on another trod back to the saddle: this crosses the track above the western end of the tarn and on beneath the lower knoll. Rise a few feet to its crest where outcrops make a fine foreground. A pathless few minutes see you drop north-west off the grassy end, avoiding craggy ground to your right: easy grass slopes lead down to the track left earlier. Turn right on a charming course round the grassy fellside, dropping to a wall corner but then continuing on. Fording a small stream it drops left through bracken to approach a gate with an old rail bridge behind, but as the track swings more right go left back over the stream to a gate in the wall. A green way heads off with a wall: through a bridle-gate at the end an old walled way takes over around colourful terrain, notably when a reedy pool forms a foreground to the Howgills. Just yards beyond a wall corner a gate empties onto an access track. Jordan Lane is just to the left and leads back to the main road near the start. However, a permissive path goes through the gate opposite, over an old rail bridge and left along the old Clapham-Tebay line. This is a lovely few minutes, with the Lune closing in below. Approaching a stone-arched bridge bear left to a gate to join an enclosed bridleway: this rises left to rejoin Jordan Lane. Turn right on its grassy-stripped, hedgerowed course, (a Roman road) back to the A683. The start is just minutes further.

The Howgill Fells from Holme Knott

7 KILLINGTON

4 miles from Killington

A lovely hamlet above a quiet corner of the Lune

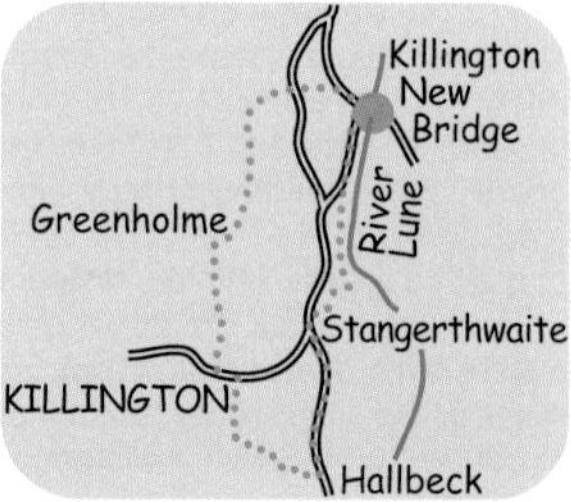

Start Killington New Bridge (GR: 622907), parking on east side Map OS Explorer OL2, Yorkshire Dales South/West OS Explorer OL19, Howgill Fells & Upper Eden Valley

The splendid arched bridge straddles a fine length of the Lune much favoured by canoeists. Cross it to a junction and take the road left. After merging with the river it soon rises away, here take a stile in the hedge on the left. A faint path heads off through a few trees, closing in on the river and crossing a sidestream to leave the wood. The path runs downstream to a hut at a weir, just past which a grassy way runs to restored buildings at Kingfisher Mill. Pass between them and out to the drive at the front. As it swings right to pass two houses, advance on across the lawn to resume downstream. At the end of the garden a stile puts you back above the river, though soon the ways part as the enclosed path runs a little higher and pleasantly on to join a driveway. This runs parallel with the river to the hamlet of Stangerthwaite. With the farm in front and a splendid abandoned house on your left, bear right on a narrow lane running a hedgerowed course to rise to a minor crossroads.

Go left, dropping at the end to Hallbeck hamlet. Just over the bridge is a bungalow, alongside which an enclosed green way heads off. This narrows pleasantly before emerging: between trees and wall it rises away, then curves faintly right to re-approach the stream. A stile puts you into its wooded confines and a path rises along the edge, running on and leaving by a stile ahead. Cross to another in front, from where an enclosed path runs a fine course rising to a junction of like ways. Turn right on this splendid, broader way into Killington. Rise left up the road, soon taking an access road right to cross a lively beck to a fascinating corner between the hall of 1640 with an older ruined part and All Saints church. Keep on to the top house, where go right on a garden edge, crossing a stream to a stile into a field. Rise away to a stile above, and continue to a gate at the top: pause to look back over the hamlet and the Lune Valley to Middleton Fell. Keep on the fenceside to a gate in it just before it starts to drop away. The view now reveals the splendid Howgill Fells ahead. From the gate rise left to the top of the domed pasture, levelling out to pass the top of a small wood. At the end ignore a gate in the corner above and instead take a track that forms to its right.

This runs on a hedgeside dropping towards Greenholme. Before it take a stile on the left and cross to a gate: just beyond, a track runs to meet an old green lane above the farm. Drop right to a gate into it, and briefly head away on the drive. Almost at once double back left to a gate/stile, and back across the field to a gate in a wall. Continue to a gate/stile at the far end, then on beneath a bracken bank into Cowby Wood. A faint path drops through it, crossing a stile before the trees thin. At the corner ahead the path forks by a waterfall. From the stile on your right drop briefly down the field to a fence-stile on the left. This forces an immediate crossing of the stream, then across towards Grassrigg farm. A fence-stile ahead puts you onto its drive: turn right onto a back road. From a gate opposite cross to a facing gate, then down a larger field to a stile in a hedge onto another back road: drop right to finish.

Killington New Bridge

8 CASTLEY FLANKS

$3\frac{3}{4}$ miles from Howgill

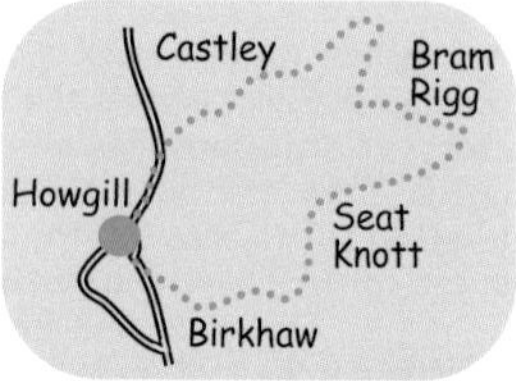

Splendid green ways on the lower flanks of the delectable western Howgills

Start Howgill church (GR: 633950), below gated road $2\frac{1}{2}$ miles on Howgill Lane from Sedbergh, parking alongside
Map OS Explorer OL19, Howgill Fells & Upper Eden Valley
Access Open Access, see page 5

Dating from 1838, the little church of the Holy Trinity stands beside Chapel Beck, the main western drainer of the fells, and is the heart of Howgill's scattered farming community. Back on Howgill Lane turn right, steeply uphill to reach the drive to Blandsgill. With immediate views to the western Howgills, take an adjacent stile and head up the fieldsides by Smithy Beck to a small gate into the yard at Birkhaw. Turn left past the buildings and a broad track heads away through trees, then rises up a couple of fieldsides to a gate at the top. It then runs left along a wallside to a gate onto the open fell. Heading away by the wall on your left, it quickly rises to a brow with a magnificent view into the fells.

The track slowly curves away from the wall beneath the knoll of Seat Knott and along its flank for some while (absorbing tracks from below) before slanting down to ford Swarth Greaves Beck and Bram Rigg Beck either side of a sheepfold. Doubling back up the other side ignore a grassy branch right, and a little further take a level grassy branch left. This runs on, dropping slightly through bracken to fade on a gentle knoll near the foot of Bram Rigg. Bear right, possibly on a faint trod, to quickly be looking down on Chapel Beck. To the right is a clump of reeds, where you look down on a very distinct sheeptrod heading right. Drop onto this and go right, quickly joined by a lower one where you must exercise caution above a perilous landslip. Otherwise the trod runs a typical level course through bracken, only fading at the end as the steeper slopes recede. Advance just a little further to meet an old grassy track slanting down from the right, and turn down this the short way to Calf Beck. The track fords it and doubles back left a few yards to meet a green track descending the long spur of White Fell. Go left on this to ford Long Rigg Beck, after which this well-made way curves up beneath Castley Knotts. Pause to look back at the fairest of scenes, with the western ridges of The Calf's group interlocking between deep-cut side becks. Of the similarly appointed tops, it is The Calf itself that, surprisingly, appears of least significance. The track rises to a gate off the fell by sheep pens, then runs an enclosed course to quickly reach Castley Farm in its enviable setting.

Turn left down the drive into the farm, dropping right to a yard by the house. Here take the right-hand of two gates below and slant away down a fenceside. Through a gate in the wall at the end rise to a small gateway on the brow just ahead, then with a steep bank below bear right across to a ladder-stile. Head towards the farm ahead, dropping down to cross a trickle and on to a track, but take the left-hand of two gates ahead and bear left of all buildings to find a stile onto the narrow road at Gateside. Turn down this for the final few minutes back to the start.

The Calf group from above Castley

9 Crook of Lune

3½ miles from Howgill

A superb length of the Lune leads to a classic old bridge

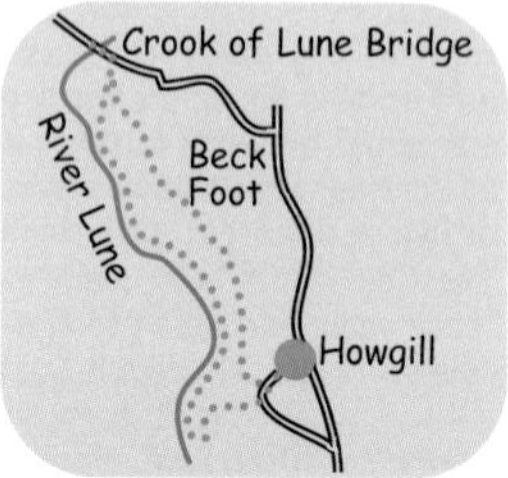

Start *Howgill church (GR: 633950) below gated road 2½ miles on Howgill Lane from Sedbergh, parking alongside*
Map *OS Explorer OL19, Howgill Fells & Upper Eden Valley*

The little church of the Holy Trinity stands beside Chapel Beck, and is the heart of Howgill's farming community. Head along its side road to a group of dwellings, and remain on the road climbing away. On the brow it meets a farm track, with big Howgills views to the left. Turn right to descend to Thwaite Farm, with the Lune and Lowgill Viaduct beyond. Entering its yard go left between barns, at the far end finding a stile behind the last building. A bank drops steeply towards the Lune, but for now go left along the top, dropping at the end on a path to a footbridge on Smithy Beck in front of Hole House. Don't cross but turn right on the Dales Way path to a stile out of the trees and along to the River Lune. Turn right to trace it upstream through a large pasture below Thwaite Farm. Initially very narrow between rocks, the river soon opens out with wide, stony banks. Fell Head, westernmost 2000-footer of the Howgills, appears ahead, rapidly joined by a fuller entourage.

A footbridge crosses Chapel Beck and the river remains in close company, its part-wooded bank rich in springtime flora. With Crook of Lune Farm up to the right the path is sent right to a gate just ahead, and slants up to a grassy track at the fieldtop: you shall return here after a brief detour to Crook of Lune Bridge. For now go left on the faint track to a gate/stile onto the bend of a narrow road descending to the bridge, where a grassy bank offers a spot to repose. This beautiful structure curves at each end and inclines to a narrow crest: dating back possibly almost 500 years, it carries only local traffic yet is within a half-mile of the M6. Up behind is

Lowgill, one-time railway junction where trains leaving the viaduct would enter Lowgill Station to join the main line. Above, motorway traffic and express trains now thunder in parallel into the Lune Gorge.

Return up the lane and along the green track, this time going on to the farm. Pass through a couple of gates into the yard and out on the drive climbing away, but at the first bend leave by a gate on the right. Head along the wallside with the Howgills on better view now, and when it drops away slant to the hedge below. At the far corner pass through a gate onto a track, then left through another on the quickly fading track. In the field drop down to meet a fence on your right, and on to a corner stile. Go left through a gate and a track drops to the unkempt environs of Beck Foot. Go briefly downstream with Ellergill Beck, over a footbridge, and rise over a track just above. This quickly puts you onto another track going right, away from the farm. Quickly reaching a gate don't pass through but take a small gate on the left, and rise to a good track just above. Go right on this across a lengthy pasture to Tarnhouse Barn at the end. The track fades but use a gate right of the barn. Head directly away on another wallside track, and when the wall turns off follow the track to a house. A short enclosed way leads to the front, where ignore the drive and take a wall-stile on the left. Cross the pasture to the houses ahead, and a footbridge on Chapel Beck. This is a nice corner with an old mill upstream. Across, wind up between the houses back onto the road, with the church just to the left.

Crook of Lune Bridge

10 Fell Head

3½ miles
from Fairmile Gate

An uncomplicated ascent of a 2000-foot fell: a clear day is needed

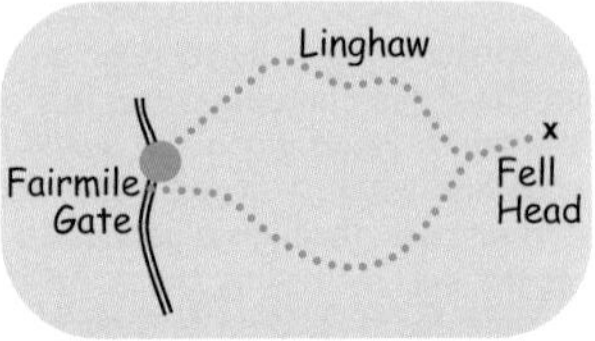

Start Fairmile Gate (GR: 629978), parking area on brow north of bridge (4½ miles north of Sedbergh)
Map OS Explorer OL19, Howgill Fells & Upper Eden Valley
Access Open Access, see page 5

Fairmile Gate is on a minor road 3 miles south of the A685 at Low Borrow Bridge, and is the point where Fairmile Road leaves the open fell to become Howgill Lane. This was on the Roman road to the camp at nearby Low Borrow Bridge: the name survives though a cattle-grid long since replaced the gate. Fell Head rises directly above, set back behind the slopes of Linghaw. From the top end of the parking area a distinct green path rises through bracken to the north of Dry Gill towards the intimidating slopes of Linghaw. When the bracken ends take a well-earned break to savour super views over the Lune Valley: there is a particularly good stretch of the river immediately up-dale, as it emerges from the Lune Gorge. Far beyond is a Lakeland skyline featuring the Coniston Fells, with the Scafells' defile of Mickledore slotting neatly in further right - on a day of excellent clarity.

As this steepest section finally ends a few fainter yards precede a broader green way curving up to the right: it steepens again as one of several parallel grooves rise to ease out on approaching the grassy felltop. Simply rise up onto easing ground to meet a broad grass track rising from the left: gentler slopes see you gain the unmarked grassy top of Linghaw (1640ft/500m). Fell Head returns to the scene, hopefully looking more attainable now: the summit cairn sits back to the left of the western top. Over to the left are the wilder upper recesses of Carlingill.

Turn right on the broad grassy way to quickly drop to the intervening saddle, and ignoring cross-paths take the most obvious, initially broader path directly up onto Blake Ridge, Fell Head's north-western spur. A delectable path winds invitingly up to gain the western top of Fell Head, either directly or on the old path first swinging right. It is marked by a small cairn and a junction with a broader path coming up from the right: your return route is down this. It is now but two minutes along and slightly up the broad, inviting ridge to the more substantial summit cairn. This last stage enjoys the benefits of the new view ahead to the high Calf skyline. At 2100ft/640m Fell Head is the second of the five Howgills' 2000-footers, and its 'outpost' situation makes it a superb all-round viewpoint, not only for its numerous neighbours, but also looking down on the Lune Gorge, across to the Whinfell Ridge and Lakeland.

Return to the western cairn and this time remain on the broad path slanting left, commencing a superb, very direct descent down this uniform south-western spur. Finally easing out, a thinner right fork remains on the now broad ridge. Crossing a traversing path that doubles back right, keep on your broadening path to resume a gentler descent. This fades with the intake wall in view and Whin's farm below it. Simply bear right down grassy slopes to where the wall meets the well-defined ravine of Fairmile Beck. A thin path at the wall corner runs between it and the gill, slanting down into it further along and then crossing it for the final minute back along the bracken flank to the road just beneath the start.

Carlin Gill from Linghaw

11 Carlingill Ravines

4½ miles from Carlingill

A dry, clear day is needed for this adventure into a hidden gill: time-consuming and not for the faint-hearted

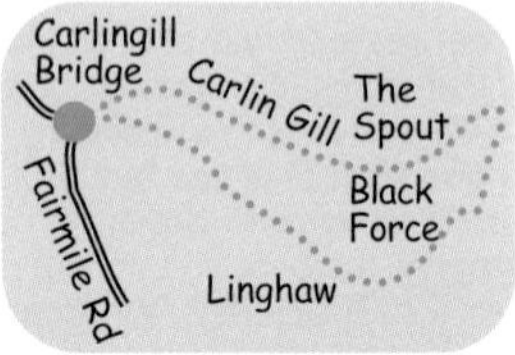

Start *Carlingill Bridge (GR: 624995), parking area to south, on Fairmile Road 5½ miles north of Sedbergh*
Map *OS Explorer OL19, Howgill Fells & Upper Eden Valley*
Access *Open Access,* *see page 5*

From the arched bridge follow Carlingill Beck upstream, a little path materialising to remain largely evident all the way, often on a little terrace above the beck. As the slopes increasingly close in, at the second inflowing gill on the right (Small Gill), the valley narrows markedly. With no obvious means of progress, cross to the opposite bank: a rough wall of scree tumbles to the deep gill, but after a brief pull a path is found to traverse cautiously across. Its return to the floor of the gill coincides with the spectacular moment of arrival at the foot of the ravine of Black Force. This is a series of tumbling little falls throughout the full length of a dark walled ravine. Keeping faith with the floor of Carlin Gill there seems no obvious way again, but a little path tackles the bouldery environs, in or on the very bank. At a rock-walled impasse it crosses the gill which soon bends right to pass a lovely waterslide. This absorbing path is then halted all too soon at the impasse of The Spout. This stunning waterfall is not fully seen until penetrating to the limit of exploration: well-named, it pours into a colourful amphitheatre.

Escape by crossing the beck to a choice of steep, grassy pull or cleaner scramble up tilted rock: either demands caution, while the latter earns an even more intimate view of The Spout. On the flank above turn right to roughly trace the upper stream through its easing ravine to approach the hollow of Blakethwaite Bottom. After Carlin Gill, this basin is a contrastingly spacious upland. Reaching a confluence, cross the thin left branch and curve right around the little tongue to meet a clearer path, there doubling back to cross the main arm of the beck (Great Ulgill Beck). Now take the right-hand of two slender ways heading away: a faint, steep little pull eases out to a gentle rise to run more clearly along, aiming for the unmistakable head of Black Force. The mercurial path runs high above the gorge of upper Carlin Gill to arrive at the calm upper reaches above Black Force. Slanting down to cross Little Ulgill Beck the path doubles back right up the short slope to a knoll revealing The Spout again. Ignore a broader path rising left towards Fell Head, and remain on the path setting forth on a fine traverse high above Carlin Gill around to a saddle linking the minor top of Linghaw (right) with its parent fell (left). Grand views range from the peaks of Lakeland to the waters of Morecambe Bay.

At this crossroads of green ways turn right to surmount the unmarked grassy summit of Linghaw (1640ft/500m) and remain on the broad green way slanting off to the right (north-west), initially gently and then more firmly down the hill. With the Lune Gorge outspread below the finish is a fairly obvious one, the farmer's quad track tracing the extended shoulder of the fell almost all the way back to the start. It fades somewhat on a gentler knoll towards the bottom, but picks up again before fading on flatter terrain just short of the road.

The Spout, Carlingill

12 WINDER

3¼ miles
from Sedbergh

A classic little fellwalk, and the finest introduction to Sedbergh and the Howgills

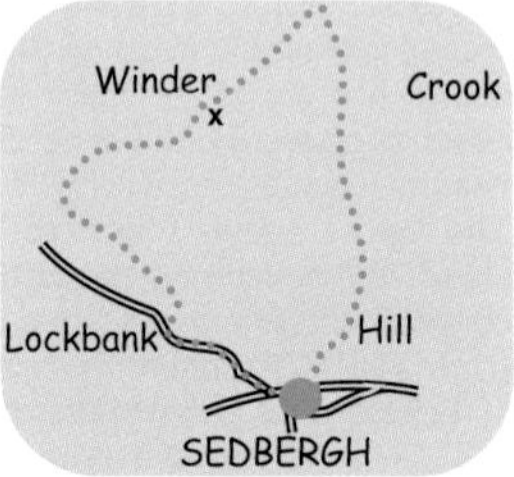

Start *Town centre (GR: 658921), car parks*
Map *OS Explorer OL19, Howgill Fells & Upper Eden Valley*
Access *Open Access,* *see page 5*

Leave the main street by Joss Lane rising between the United Reformed Church and the main car park. It swings up to the right: 'to the fell' signs ease the way out of town as it swings right through modern housing. From its demise at a gate a farm road to Hill takes over, while your way slants to a stile at the top corner of the field. An enclosed path climbs to rise alongside Settlebeck Gill to gain the open fell at a kissing-gate. Already there is a smashing prospect over the town and its attendant dales and hills, with Baugh Fell, Whernside, Great Coum and Middleton Fell prominent.

With a choice of paths take the green one slanting up behind a seat, quickly doubling back right for a delightful slant high above the colourful gill. Slowly deflected away by a sidestream, the path reaches an upland basin on Winder's flank, with neighbouring Crook across the gill and parent fell Arant Haw seen further ahead. The way continues up, steepening again and rising to ease out on a knoll where Arant Haw appears fully ahead. This is a stunning moment, as a clear day reveals the Lakeland Fells to the west. Turning your back on the higher Howgills, double back left on a green carpet bound for Winder. A slight descent precedes the steadiest of rises (ignore any branches) along the broad ridge, over grassy knolls to Winder's Ordnance Survey column and view indicator at 1551ft/473m. This neat top boasts a superb panorama, including a fine prospect up the Lune Gorge to the western Howgills. Garsdale and Dentdale are both seen burrowing deep into the higher Dales fells. Drop a little towards Sedbergh for an intimate bird's-eye picture, fittingly as Winder is regarded as the town's 'special' fell.

Leave by a path striking west towards the Lune, an outstanding green way that descends to within a stone's throw of the intake wall. Keep left at a bend above the wall and a lesser but clear path contours on, over several minor streams as Sedbergh appears ahead. A broad way comes in from the left as you slant down to finally join the wall. This is shadowed down to a gate off the fell behind Lockbank Farm: drop down to a short green way into the yard, emerging via the farm drive (a permissive path) onto Howgill Lane, turning left to re-enter town.

Winder from Sedbergh

Left: Garsdale from the ascent path

13 BRIGFLATTS

4¼ miles from Sedbergh

Charming riverbank walking and a Quaker landmark

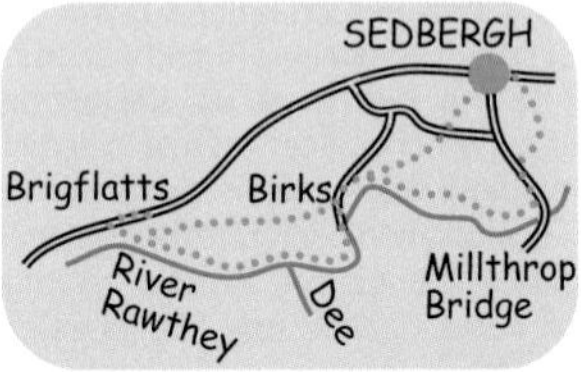

Start *Town centre (GR: 658921), car park*

Map *OS Explorer OL19, Howgill Fells & Upper Eden Valley*

Go west on the main street to the church and turn down the Dent road, quickly taking a path right between churchyard and Sedbergh School's cricket pitch. This famous public school counts many famous names amongst its old boys, including record-breaking England rugby caption Will Carling. Meeting a track at the end, bear left on a still surfaced path along the back of the pavilion. Cross over a drive to a kissing-gate into a field, and with the frontage of the school to the right, head straight down to a kissing-gate onto a road. Cross straight over and away on a track past more sports fields. Reaching a barn take a kissing-gate on the right, and a path crosses to the far end of the field. Curving round beneath a lone house, keep straight on past it to a kissing-gate onto a narrow lane.

Go left past attractive cottages at Birks, and on the bend beyond take a kissing-gate on the right and bear left to a wall corner. Keep on the wallside to a kissing-gate at the end, straight on a further field, then bear right to a pair of gates flanking a track. Continue to an underpass in the railway embankment ahead. To the right this transforms into a cutting to approach Sedbergh's station on this former Clapham-Tebay branch. Through it, cross to the left-hand of two gates in a wall, then on through two fields to emerge into Brigflatts. Opposite is a Quaker burial ground, while just to the left in the beautiful setting of this old hamlet is an historic Friends' Meeting House. With a 1675 datestone it still serves its original role, and its peaceful interior oozes calm. High Brigflatts, opposite, bears a 1743 datestone. Return along the access road out to the A684, and go left for a few minutes as far as a kissing-gate on the left. A path doubles back to run above a wooded bank of the

Rawthey, dropping down at the rear of Brigflatts Farm to join the river through open pasture. This leads unerringly to Birks Mill, enjoying superb river scenery en route: additionally you encounter an old rail bridge, with the line giving good views to the nearest Howgill Fells, and also a tree-shrouded confluence of the inflowing River Dee.

At Birks Mill ignore a footbridge on the river and follow the road back up to Birks. Retrace steps to the fieldpath where you entered, but this time bear right by the house on a path dropping to a stile alongside the river. Trace the Rawthey as far as the next stile, then bear left up the side of a small wood, through a gateway to the brow of the hill. Fine views of the Howgills are enjoyed alongside a ruined folly. Pass left of the wood corner and on to a kissing-gate into the trees. The path heads away to fork alongside a walled trench: bear right through this, emerging to resume above the river to leave the wood by a small gate at the end. Advance on the length of the field to a gate/stile at the far end onto a road at Millthrop Bridge. Go left towards town, but on levelling out take a stile on the right, and a path crosses the field to rise to a corner stile. Ascend outside the wall of the large Winder House, onto a brow revealing the whole town beneath Winder. Kissing-gates take you across its drive and down a fenceside onto an access road, Vicarage Lane. Advance straight along this to re-enter town.

Friends Meeting House, Brigflatts

14 — TWO RIVERS

4 miles from Sedbergh

A delightful stroll at the feet of two valleys

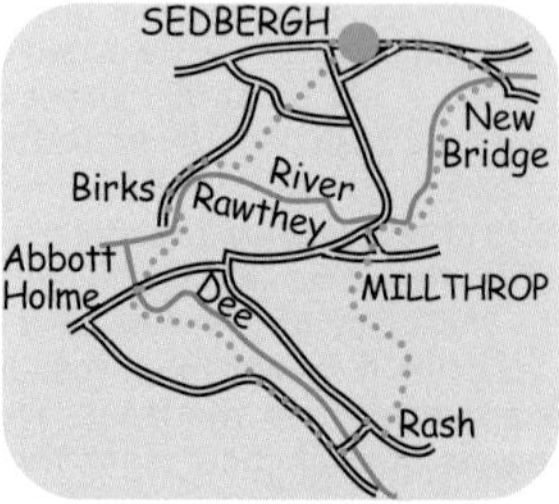

Start Town centre (GR: 658921), car parks
Map OS Explorer OL2, Yorkshire Dales South/West
OS Explorer OL19, Howgill Fells & Upper Eden Valley

For the first stage to Birks, please refer to the opening paragraph of Walk 14. Follow the road left past attractive cottages at Birks and down to its terminus at Birks Mill. Cross the Rawthey by a footbridge at a lovely section of river: up the bank opposite, turn downstream. From a corner stile the path runs through woodland, quickly climbing to a small gate out of the trees. With the river gone, the thin path heads away to another gate just ahead. Emerging onto Sedbergh golf course, watch for flying balls and bear right, crossing to a broad gap in a hedgeline, then continue to a gate/stile onto a back road. Go briefly right to Abbott Holme Bridge, across which take a stile on the left. This admits to another section of the disjointed course, again being wary of flying balls. This again is a lovely section of river, the Dee passing beneath its shapely final bridge prior to being swallowed up by the Rawthey.

Head upstream, quickly escaping the course at a stile. Beyond a tiny stream the route bears left, rising steadily along a scant row of trees. At the end is a stile into rougher pasture, and a path slants gently up the steepening bank above the river to a small gate in the wall at the top. This brow offers a super prospect with the Dee backed by the Howgills, also Wild Boar Fell, Swarth Fell, Baugh Fell, Rise Hill, Whernside, and Combe Scar overlooking lower Dentdale. A delectable green way heads off above a dense bracken bank, tracing the wall all the way to a stile onto another back road. Go left on this traffic-free way, the surroundings of the nearby river remain idyllic. First buildings reached are an old mill with millstones still lined up outside, and the humble Dent Foot Methodist Chapel. At Rash Bridge just beyond, cross the river and climb to the Dent road. Go right to the farm buildings of Rash, passing a milestone advising the distance to Sedbergh. Take a gate on the left and a thin path climbs to a wall corner, continuing up to a gate/stile: this is the only real climb of the walk. Continue up the next field, bearing left to find a stile at the very top corner onto a lovely green bridleway. Go left, and at an early fork remain on the top one which soon swings right to the brow. This high point of the walk trades Dentdale for the Rawthey scene once more, as Sedbergh and the Howgill Fells return to view.

A bridle-gate admits onto the old golf course. Take the path straight ahead, crossing a track which is rejoined and followed away. This soon drops more steeply with a wall, becoming a stony lane to descend into Millthrop. Turn right through the compact hamlet to a T-junction, passing attractive millworkers' cottages and a curiously-shaped Methodist chapel of 1889, with one of 1888 next-door: both are now houses. Go left at the junction back down onto the Dent road by the Rawthey, just short of Millthrop Bridge. Don't cross but take a small gate on the right to head upstream, soon enjoying a wide spell with a hedge over to right. The path stays near the riverbank to reach New Bridge. Cross this and go left onto a path parallel to run by school grounds and along to a driveway to rejoin the road, following the pathway back into town.

Haytime in lower Dentdale

15 Rawthey's Bank

3^{1}2 miles
from Sedbergh

Gentle riverbank and field walking under the Howgills' lower flanks

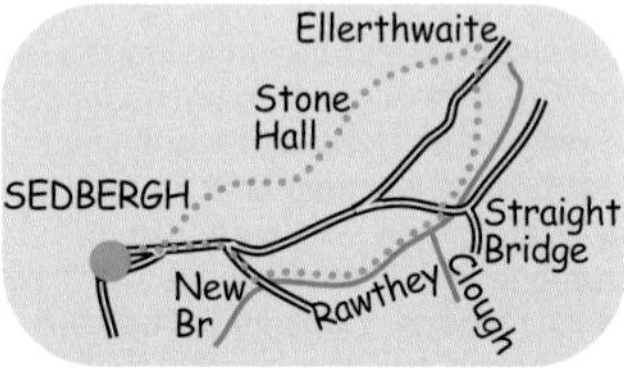

Start Town centre (GR: 658921), car parks
Map OS Explorer OL19, Howgill Fells & Upper Eden Valley

Leave the eastern end of the main street by continuing on to where the Hawes road forks right, and follow it to quickly reach New Bridge. Don't cross but turn upstream, a good path shadowing the river to shortly emerge into the open. Ahead are the broad shoulders of Baugh Fell, with Wild Boar Fell's top set further back left. Directly above you is a grouping of the lower Howgill Fells. Simply remain on the riverbank all the way to Straight Bridge. En route footbridges take you over two sidestreams, while a curious down-ladder drops you down the foot of a small wooded bank. Just before reaching Straight Bridge comes a fine moment at a confluence with the inflowing River Clough, from Garsdale: a nice waterfall tumbles over ledges just upstream.

A stile puts you onto the road by the single-arched bridge. Cross the road, not the bridge, and resume as before along the riverbank. This time the spell soon ends: beyond the next stile the way is forced up above a wooded bank, with the boisterous confluence of Hebblethwaite Hall Gill darkly below. Suddenly the river is now far below, and heading on with the fence the sprawling farm of Buck Bank appears just ahead. A green track soon forms to lead into the yard, bearing right between the main buildings to emerge onto a road. Turn right a short way to the next house, Ellerthwaite, and take a stile on the left to rise outside its garden. From a stile at the top slant left to the top edge of an old wall, and crossing a stream behind it aim to the far end of the field where a stile awaits. Another stream is crossed to advance to a ladder-stile just ahead, then cross directly to the farm at Hollin Hall. A gate puts you into its yard, and immediately after the house with a 1712 datestone on its porch, take a gate on the right and cross a field to a footbridge on a sidestream. Now follow the fieldside away to the next farm, Stone House, an old gem with a three-storey porch. Just beyond a barn a gate puts you into its confines. Go left over the cattle-grid and out along the drive. Great Coum and Middleton Fell are well seen ahead beyond hidden lower Dentdale.

Another driveway soon merges, and just a little further take a gate/stile in a recess on the right on a bend. Follow a wall left to a footbridge crossing Ashbeck Gill, and cross to an outer corner just ahead. Cross the field to a gate/stile onto a rough access road, and follow this right up to the hamlet of Underbank. Rise left to the end of the buildings, and an enclosed cart track heads away. This runs a charming leafy course, at the end reaching a house where a firmer drive begins: on the left is Baliol School. Remain on the access road (Thorns Lane) dropping away, but as modern housing starts on the right, take an enclosed path between house and field edge. Up above is the wooded prow of Castlehaw, a distinctive mound that is the site of an ancient motte and bailey. At the end the path crosses to a stile onto the main road on the edge of town, going right to finish.

Sedbergh church

16 DOWBIGGIN

4¼ miles from Sedbergh

A lovely river and a stunning ravine, with sweeping views of the Howgill Fells

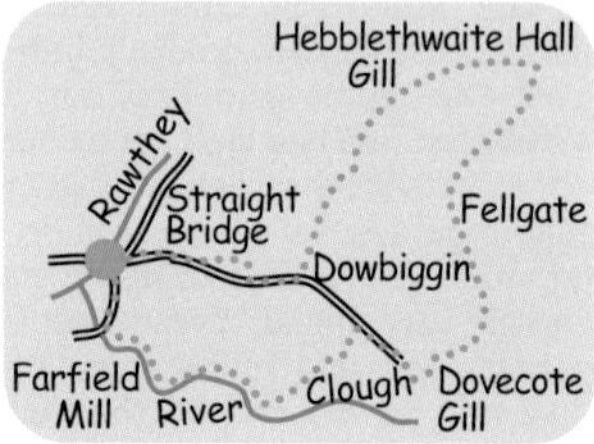

Start *Straight Bridge (GR: 676923), parking area a mile east of town*

Map *OS Explorer OL19, Howgill Fells & Upper Eden Valley*

Access *Open Access,* *see page 5*

Cross the bridge and turn right on a narrow lane that winds round to Garsdale Bridge. On the other bank is Farfield Mill, an arts and heritage centre with café. Don't cross but take a stile on the left to trace the River Clough upstream. Above a wooded bank the path descends to the river, and adheres to its winding course for a delightful section of superior river scenery. Just past a foot-bridge you are deflected up by a wooded bank: the path maintains its rise up the pasture to a stile before a marshy enclosure. Bearing left here at an invisible fork, a clearer track is joined and skirts round to the left, swinging left to a gate. Here go right to the next gate where a short stony, enclosed way climbs to Dowbiggin Lane.

Turn right on its narrow course to a drive at Dovecote Gill. Take the cart track right, winding down to cross a stream and steeply up into a field. A grassy continuation rises away, swinging left at the top to where an old track comes up from the house. With an old sunken way at right-angles, follow this right up to a gate in the wall at the top, onto the open fell at the remains of a limekiln. Rise left on a thin path above the intake wall to meet a track at the head of Dovecote Gill's secret ravine. Cross and continue along: a spell away from the wall sees you near it again at Fellgate Farm, a potentially messy corner. A track comes out from it to keep you on the fell, escaping moistness to cut another corner of the wall by ignoring a left branch. The way rises to rejoin the wall but largely fades. Forge on between the wall and an old limekiln: old tracks in improving grassy surrounds lead to a brow with a Howgills panorama. Close in on the wall as it approaches Hebblethwaite Hall Gill, soon reaching a gate (with a reedy pool behind) where you leave the fell. First the highlight of the walk beckons, going a minute further for a closer look at the scarred wall of the ravine. The gorge is carved through walls of slabby rock where the gill vacates bare moor for rich woodland. A projecting slender grassy rib invites an airy stance, though caution is required if youngsters are roaming loose!

Through the gate follow a grass track left of a distinct bank. As it fades press on along the brow, then down through a gateway in an old wall and left over another brow. Dropping more steeply at the end the track becomes enclosed to run to the old farm at Sarthwaite. Rise left to a gate and follow a grassy track across to a corner gate (ignore a stile above). It continues to a barn, where from a gate on the right descend the hedgeside to a bridle-gate and miniature arched footbridge. Head away with the hedge on your left to a corner gate, then drop to a house below: gates on its left put you on Dowbiggin Lane. Turn right, but after passing a house take a drive right: part way on take a gate on the left to follow a hedge away towards the far end where a stile/plank bridge put you on the other side of the stream. Continue down to the bottom where a stile returns you to the lane. Go right to finish.

Hebblethwaite Hall Gill

17 River Clough

3¾ miles
from Garsdale

A gentle stroll through an unsung valley, with a lengthy riverbank conclusion

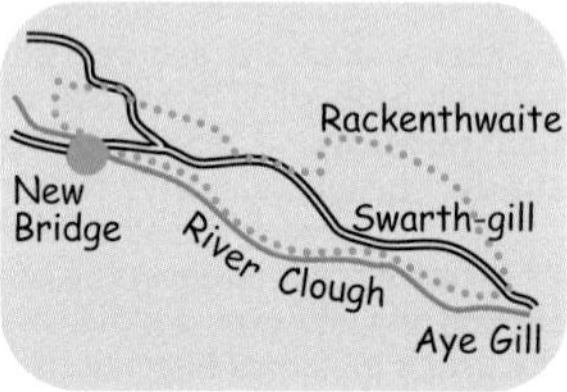

Start New Bridge (GR: 713906), parking alongside, where Hawes road crosses river almost 4 miles from Sedbergh
Map OS Explorer OL2, Yorkshire Dales South/West
OS Explorer OL19, Howgill Fells & Upper Eden Valley

Garsdale is probably the least known of any valley in the National Park, certainly for its size: its river is the Clough. On the upstream side of the bridge steps lead down to a plank bridge, and a grass track heads downstream as far as the field end. Here turn right on the track away from the river (for now) to a corner gate. Approaching a barn don't enter, instead turn right along a tree-fringed fieldside to a stile in a line of trees at the end. Keep on, and when the wall turns off bear right to a gate in another wall. Go briefly left with it to a gate back through it in the corner, and cross a tapering enclosure to a gate onto a back road at Lindsey Fold Farm. Go right a short way, and on ascending from a dip to a brow take a drive on the left (Bellow Hill). Follow it as far as the first gate, but then turn right along the wallside to a corner stile. Up behind is Baugh Fell, a mighty hill that dominates the walk. Continue with the wall, later veering right to a stile and tiny stream. Now cross to a stile ahead just above a house at Pike Hill. Turn down the drive onto the main road, and go left with care for a quarter-mile.

Just past the house at Birkrigg take a stile on the left and follow a wall away to a drive. Turn left up it to a farm, rising right of it on a green way to a barn. Pass along the front and out into a field, crossing beneath the wall to a stile and tiny stream, and on again to a wall-stile. Through a gate behind cross to the right of farm buildings at West Rackenthwaite to join the drive.

Turn up it to the house, along the front to a stile into a sloping field. Slant down to a gate just yards short of the end to join the East Rackenthwaite drive just behind. Again go left up towards the yard, but take a gate to the right of the first barn. Head across the field to find a wall-stile part hidden beyond scrub, then slant down to a small gate in the next wall. Now drop right to a gate behind a house, taking the left-most gate and down the house side. From a gate in front a nice enclosed pathway drops into trees, swinging right at the bottom and along to a gate back onto the main road opposite a stone-arched bridge at Aygill.

Turn right for less than a minute to a stile on the left, and cross the field centre towards the river. A gate and stream precede a stand of trees keeping you briefly away from the Clough, but from a stile at the end you are firmly planted on the riverbank the entire way back to New Bridge. Close by a farm bridge there are good glimpses of white-walled, three-storey Swarthgill House. Squeezing through narrow sections here leads to big open pastures. Further, a stile puts you up onto a driveway at another farm bridge. Though you don't cross it, the shell on your left across is a former Wesleyan Methodist Chapel of 1863. Follow the drive briefly to where it turns right for the adjacent road, and here use a gate to retain the riverbank for the final pasture before a stile sends an enclosed section back to New Bridge.

Swarthgill House

18 CAUTLEY SPOUT

2¾ miles
from Cautley

A justifiably famous corner of the Howgills, much of it on display before you even start the walk

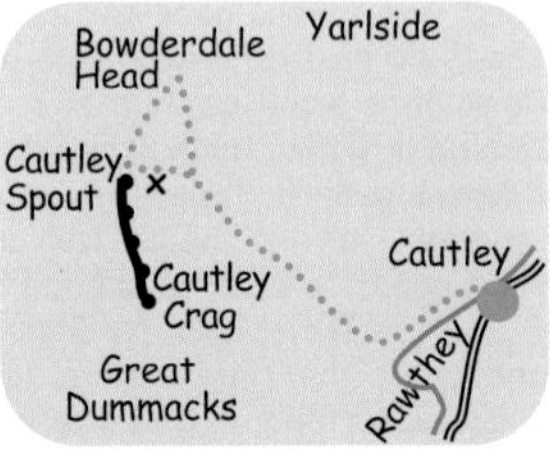

Start Cross Keys Inn (GR: 698969), parking area alongside
Map OS Explorer OL19, Howgill Fells & Upper Eden Valley
Access Open Access, *see page 5*

Cautley Crag and Spout combine to form the grandest scene in the Howgill Fells. The steep crag extends for the best part of a mile to an abrupt end at the Spout, a series of waterfalls which tumble in rapid succession for several hundred feet to the valley floor. The Cross Keys is a temperance inn offering welcome refreshments. Cautley has no definable centre, just a scattering of farms, dwellings and a church along the Sedbergh road.

By the parking area is a footbridge over the Rawthey. Pause here to appraise Great Dummacks downstream: this is the fell that boasts Cautley Crag as its own. Across, a good path heads away. Ignoring an early branch right, follow this broad, level path downstream above the Rawthey, quickly swinging in to the prized amphitheatre beneath Cautley Crag. Passing above a footbridge on Cautley Holme Beck, the path is infallibly drawn towards the base of the falls, surmounting a gentle spur that undulates along to the foot of the ravine. Here the path forks, the gentler right branch being your return route. The left branch crosses a tiny sidestream to tackle the steep climb by the gill. You quickly reach the start of a stone path, superbly engineered to make life easier in addition to its main purpose of preventing erosion. It winds cleverly up above the ravine: caution is urged when peering into the lower fall, which is partly obscured by hardy foliage. Pausing to look back, Wild Boar Fell, Swarth Fell and Baugh Fell form a sombre mountain skyline.

Further up, the upper falls are free of obstruction and can be savoured more leisurely. Virtually at the top of these the steep section ends at a small platform: the much gentler continuation left begins with a tiny rock band, but this is the point where your climb ends. So leave the main path for a short, steady traverse on a thin trod right. This partly fades but resurrects itself to soon slant down the short way to the incisive pass of Bowderdale Head, backed by the upper flanks of Yarlside. Bowderdale is a lonely valley running north for some four miles. Turning right a good path descends the other side of the tiny stream. After initial zigzags and a brief stony spell, it settles down to a mercurial descent through lower bracken to the foot of the Spout, to return the way you came.

Cautley Spout

19 Upper Rawthey

4¼ miles from Cautley

A memorable stride around the higher reaches of the beautiful River Rawthey, with stunning views of the Cautley scene

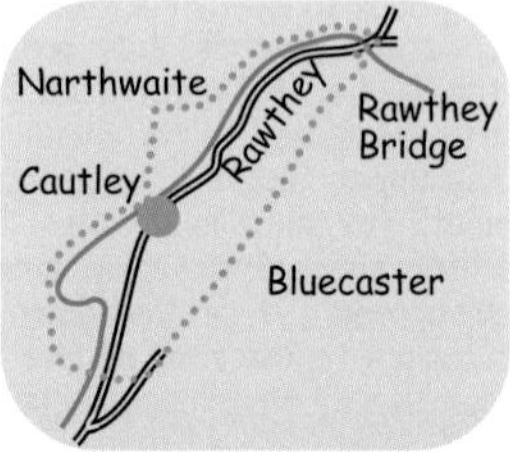

Start Cross Keys Inn (GR: 698969), parking area alongside
Map OS Explorer OL19, Howgill Fells & Upper Eden Valley

The Cross Keys is a temperance inn offering welcome refreshments: cross a footbridge over the Rawthey just above it and go straight ahead on a broad path. Within a minute fork right on another good path, continuing as a pleasant green way on the base of Ben End to a wall corner. It runs on to ford Backside Beck beneath a plantation: after heavy rain this can prove a challenge. Across, a short enclosed pull rises to Narthwaite. Cross the farmyard to the right of the house, and the drive runs steadily down the slope beyond. Ahead are Wild Boar Fell and Swarth Fell, with your return route on the flanks opposite. Just before it swings sharp right to drop to the road take a gate in front: this points the way on a lesser track concluding at a wood at the end. Through the right-hand gate ford a stream to follow a path a short way along the wood edge, quickly leaving by a ladder-stile into a field. An intermittent path runs left along its top edge outside the wood to a stile into trees at the end. A lovely path runs through this oakwood just above the river: all is preciously unspoilt hereabouts, and the Rawthey exudes all its charms in this green valley with bare fells rising on each side.

Emerging from the trees at a stile cross a brace of fields, and over a footbridge on a tiny stream to rise to a gate/stile onto the road just above Rawthey Bridge. Turn right to cross it, and a few strides further take a gate on the left, from where a track heading away almost at once turns right for a gentle rise to a brow. On crossing a small stream ignore a branch left, and the track now starts to run parallel with but high above the main road. On this section from Rawthey Bridge to beyond Bluecaster you enjoy a sustained march along the old road from Kirkby Stephen, once the main highway through these hills. Constructed well above the valley floor, it now forms a green promenade with outstanding views across to the eastern Howgills. Passing Bluecaster Cottage it becomes surfaced, and a little further a gate is reached at a lane-head. Immediately after it take a gate on the right to descend by a winding, sunken old way onto the main road.

Cross and head down a farm road past Wardses to bridge the Rawthey. The drive continues through a couple of fields, past an old limekiln to Cautley Thwaite Farm. Go straight on through a bridle-gate ahead, left of the buildings. Advance on the fieldside to a gate, then a clearer track runs left across a pasture to a gate right of a barn: the river is just below again. Past the barn the track runs to a gate onto the base of the open fell. Turn right through a gate, and a short enclosed way runs to Cautley Holme Beck, crossed by a foot-bridge. The banks here make a delightful spot for a final sojourn, with Cautley Crag and Spout looking magnificent as ever ahead. Advance a few strides to a broad path, and turn right on it, running just above the river to quickly return to the starting footbridge.

Cautley Crag from the Rawthey

20 WANDALE HILL

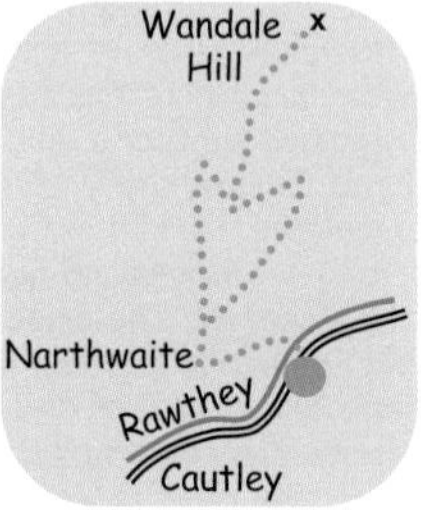

3½ miles
from Cautley

A simple ascent of an unsung grassy hill, far from human life and with outstanding mountain scenery

Start Handley's Bridge (GR: 705975), large lay-by a long half-mile north of Cross Keys
Map OS Explorer OL19, Howgill Fells & Upper Eden Valley
Access Open Access, see page 5

Go north along the road a couple of minutes to Handley's Bridge, and turn left on an unsignposted access road over the River Rawthey. This is the farm drive to Narthwaite, and swings left for a long, steady rise into the farmyard. Wandale Hill sends its long southern ridge down to the confluence of Westerdale's Backside Beck and the Rawthey, and Narthwaite occupies a fine position near the foot of this spur. Cross straight over the yard to a gate opposite, and follow the track rising to the right. Ahead are good views of Cautley Crag and neighbouring Yarlside. Remain with the right-hand wall on a part-sunken climb to the top, and a choice of bridleways and gates: you will later return to this point. Use the higher gate to follow a grassy path alongside the left-hand wall, rising steadily to a gate onto the open hill. Over to the left is the bulk of Yarlside, with its ridge running north to Kensgriff, Randygill Top and Green Bell.

Continue rising a short way on the green way, and when it levels out, double back up to the right on a similar old way, part-sunken as it slants up to meet the wall at an old sheepfold on the ridge. After the ensuing simple climb to the top you will return to this point to start a variation finish. Over to your right now are the western slopes of Wild Boar Fell and Swarth Fell. Turn left to ascend the broad grassy ridge, making a very steady, pathless ascent on easy grass to the broad felltop. A once-tiny cairn may be just a solitary stone, found towards the back at 1630ft/497m, with a tiny pool nearby. The fell-dominated panorama features the Yarlside ridge to the west; the deep trough of Uldale (upper valley of the Rawthey) straight across to the east with Wild Boar Fell, Swarth Fell and Baugh Fell behind; the limestone scars of Stennerskeugh and Fell End Clouds of Wild Boar Fell well seen under High Seat; and northwards the North Pennines. Note the well-defined line of farms and cottages on the Street, the old Sedbergh-Kirkby Stephen road under Wild Boar Fell.

Retrace your steps back to the wall, all the while fully savouring the magnificent views. Now vary the return by using the step-stile in the wall from where an improving old grassy way goes left beneath the wall, then slants down the rough pasture towards the forlorn ruin of Wandale. Splendid views look to the woods of Murthwaite Park below, across the side valley of Wandale. Here double back right on a sunken track beneath a hedge, and this same way runs on with some slight descent through several pastures to rejoin the outward route just above Narthwaite. Drop back down through the farm to finish as you began.

Yarlside and Kensgriff from under Wandale Hill

HILLSIDE GUIDES... cover much of Northern England

Other colour *Pocket Walks* guides (more in preparation)

·UPPER WHARFEDALE ·LOWER WHARFEDALE
·UPPER WENSLEYDALE ·LOWER WENSLEYDALE
·MALHAMDALE ·SWALEDALE ·RIBBLESDALE
·INGLETON/WESTERN DALES ·SEDBERGH/DENTDALE
·NIDDERDALE ·HARROGATE/KNARESBOROUGH
·BOWLAND ·AROUND PENDLE ·RIBBLE VALLEY
·AMBLESIDE/LANGDALE ·BORROWDALE
·AIRE VALLEY ·ILKLEY/WASHBURN VALLEY

Our *Walking Country* range features more great walks...

·WHARFEDALE ·MALHAMDALE ·WENSLEYDALE
·HARROGATE & the WHARFE VALLEY ·SWALEDALE
·RIPON & LOWER WENSLEYDALE ·NIDDERDALE
·THREE PEAKS ·HOWGILL FELLS ·HOWARDIAN HILLS
·TEESDALE ·EDEN VALLEY ·ALSTON & ALLENDALE

·ILKLEY MOOR ·BRONTE COUNTRY ·CALDERDALE
·PENDLE & the RIBBLE ·WEST PENNINE MOORS
·ARNSIDE & SILVERDALE ·LUNESDALE ·BOWLAND

·LAKELAND FELLS, SOUTH ·LAKELAND FELLS, EAST
·LAKELAND FELLS, NORTH ·LAKELAND FELLS, WEST

Long Distance Walks

·COAST TO COAST WALK ·CUMBRIA WAY ·DALES WAY
·LADY ANNE'S WAY ·NIDDERDALE WAY
·WESTMORLAND WAY ·FURNESS WAY
·PENDLE WAY ·BRONTE WAY ·CALDERDALE WAY

Visit www.hillsidepublications.co.uk
or write for a catalogue